I0162451

Signal Fires

Sy Margaret Baldwin

Published in the United States by Word Project
Press
of Sonora, CA

Requests for permission to make copies of any
part of this work should be submitted online at
info@wordprojectpress.com

ISBN-13: 978-0989068246
ISBN-10: 0989068242

CREDITS

Cover Design: Melody W. Baker
Front Cover Image:
From a NASA photograph of a galaxy cluster
300 million light-years away in the constellation
Pegasus.
Author Photo: Pamela A. Conners

"When Jemmy reached the shore, he lighted a signal fire, and the smoke curled up, bidding us a last and long farewell, as the ship stood on her course into the open sea."

—Charles Darwin
Voyage of the Beagle

For my sister—

Janet Elizabeth Baldwin

CONTENTS

Signal Fires

ONE

The Piano

Late afternoon. My sister sits down
at the piano, raises the hinged lid, and studies
the rows of black and white keys
spread before her—

a black and white map, an elusive code, a band
of black deer running across a snowfield.

What will flow out of her now into the world?

The piano relaxes—its many carbon-steel wires
unperturbed, its tiny hammers asleep in their berths.

And silence begins to accumulate
into a lucent blue lake—the blue of submarine
canyons and nocturnes—over
which swallows dip and veer, wide-gaped,
scooping insects out of the air.

Quietly the piano floats and reflects everything—

a moment's happiness

the calmness of the lake, a single breath

held in the beak of a swallow.

Tarifa, Andalusia

Flocks of red and chestnut finches, musical
seed-eaters, finally coming in to land, feed

in the rough grass, pause to trill from the tops
of the sand hummocks—a sound that is carried

by the wind westward to the whitewashed stones
of the windsurfer camp, to the ears of goats

browsing thistles on the hillside. It sieves
and echoes through the twisted branches

of the cork trees—a sound like the clinking
of a thousand champagne glasses.

The finch-catchers gossip, puff strong cigarettes,
breathe out blue smoke, as they settle themselves

behind the sea wall, keeping a business eye
on the entangling courses of their nets—

as I turn away, turn back to the café-bar where
a mother-of-pearl clock is striking the hours.

After the July Bombings

In the intractable tunnels I can see the glint
of soda cans. I can feel the damp cold flesh

of collapsed plastic bags caught under
muscular bundles of black cables

stapled to the tunnel walls. There are more
cameras now hidden behind billboards,

bomb-detectors at all entrances and exits,
sniffer dogs, unfriendly and non-communicative,

patrolling beneath the escalators.
There is not a lot to be said

in the intractable tunnels, so I open
my morning newspaper to the center page—

Mystery Mammal Discovered in Borneo's Forests.
Startled by the camera flash, it looks out at me—

stopped in its tracks as it bounds, minding
its own business, through the leaf mold

of the Borneo rain forest. Maybe a fox-relative,
maybe a civet cat—annoyingly its nose

was obscured by a leaf—
a rust-red coat and supple haunches,

certainly a carnivore. Maybe arboreal.
And a long, bushy tail—like the thick scarf

wrapped around the chin of the woman sitting
opposite. I remember now my dream

of the strange green glow
that seemed to emanate from my hands.

It's the hidden light of human hands I think—hands
that will enable me to escape up

to the overhead lattice of trees.

Tyneside

Last night I dreamt I was carrying
the Edwardian teapot across the Tyne Bridge
trailing the procession of mourners,

the hard breath of the horses
that were pulling my great-great-grandmother's
open coffin over the swift current of the river.

Her hands appeared like tree roots crossed
on her breast—as befitted a woman
of some standing in the community.
A black veil blinkered her eyes.

And it seemed all was as it should be
except for the half-built ships lying dormant
in the docks, and the sparrows darting away
with nothing edible in their beaks.

As I walked across the bridge
I cradled its body, its delicate spout,
its flawless translucent throat, the teapot

that had never belonged to anyone
on that hard-pressed side of the family.

Visiting the Earl of Dudley's Estate

She wasn't sure how she felt about
the huge beech trees that dwarfed her

as she walked the gravel pathways
of the Earl of Dudley's estate. For a while

she leaned against the smooth
yellow sandstone of the south façade

of his 18th-century mansion. But still
she felt tired and out of her depth.

On the other side of the ridge, the less
manicured side, she was more at home.

There she was an elderly woman
in a red cardigan resting on a bench

beside a weedy pond next to the brickworks—
a bleached lifebelt hanging on its stand

in front of her, and on the bank a pair
of preening mallards. She was herself now.

She set adrift all her years of hardship.
They floated across the pond's still surface

as if on small wooden rafts and above
them skimmed the gauzy damselflies.

Then drawn by the abrupt cry of a moorhen
in the reed bed, she looked off calmly

to where she herself seemed

to disappear in the reeds.

A Visit Home

In her white wool sweater, worn
at the elbows, she leans forward pinned

to the TV—at *last the murderer will be exposed,*
he will get what he deserves, justice will be done.

As she sits motionless, tense, hardly breathing,
I think how frail she seems—like a small

boat woven of willow stems hauled up
on the bank of a swollen river. It's late October

almost winter. Between the ceiling and roof,
in that empty space, something has taken shelter.

A mouse or bird? At night above my head
I can hear its tenuous pattering.

Pond Life

I look below the surface
of the pond to where

a great crested newt is paddling
through the billowing waterweed

of her home. So fanciful—
her warty upper-side, a sheet

of black Bubble Wrap, contrasting
with the startling Day-Glo orange

of her belly. I look below
the surface of the pond to where

the housemaid I once was
is cleaning out the fire grates

in the early morning—white grit,
a rats' nest of black cinders,

carried out by way of the servants'
passage to the ash-pile

by the vegetable beds.
There, that's done now.

She is finished with the scraping
up of scorched coals.

A light rain begins
to percolate through the ashes.

With a flick of her muscular tail,
the newt creates a tunnel

through the pondweed's

shifting veils.

By Herself

In the house a girl sits
on the floor studying illustrations

of the Seven Wonders of the World
and listening for her mother

who is in the next room dusting
and polishing the furniture. No sound.

Not even a whisper. So she lifts
a shell to her ear and listens
for the small bird singing inside.

At first only the wind, but then, as
she turns her head, she can hear its

thin tinselly song like a silver bell
ringing in the hollow of an iceberg.

All along, she thinks, it was there.

Sundews

I was surprised to find
my sister lying among the snares
of insectivorous plants, the strange
and rare sundews we had discovered
speckling the spongy moss
around the spring.
But you don't understand,
she says, *I feel at home here*
lying in the embrace of the plants,
bathing in the blue flecks of sky
dropped by the skylarks.
Must I leave her alone?
I am only twelve. She is the elder.
Perhaps I should throw in my lot
with the meadow pipits—
those shy, streaky birds winging
to their nests through the wiry grasses
that ring the bowl of moss.
As they thread their way through
they call with such light pensive whistles.
Surely the clear cold eye
of the spring will still connect us
while the plants continue their work,
the pipits fly to and fro
on their busy errands.

The Beach

Quietly, industriously, I am building a castle.
You sit in the car, far off at the back of the beach

out of the wind, knitting. To your left
the only building: a prefab shack—both shop

and snack bar, its paint stripped off
by wind-driven sand that has ridden up high

against its sides. Almost noon. A fierce shimmer.

With tin bucket and spade I am crouched
between sea edge and strandline,

my yellow dress billowing.
Behind the rippling of waves there

are subtle sounds— a flutter of wind,
the hiss of sand fleas in the tide wrack.

A hermit crab scuttles from one side
of a tide pool to the other to hide under

a frond of pink coralline seaweed.

Quick now—the tide is rising,
seawater is flooding the moat. The battlements,

the crenellated walls, the turrets, are beginning
to slump. The castle no longer exists.

Does that beach even exist anymore? Perhaps
it has blown away sand grain by sand grain.

And what of my mother? I imagine her walking
toward me bearing sandwiches and a thermos of tea.

You must be tired, I say, *you've traveled so far*

to get here

Self Portraits

Her shoes make hard tapping sounds
as she walks across the floor of the airport

terminal—then, except for that pair of
black spike-heeled shoes, she is nude,

sitting alone on a bench under a storm
of diagonal charcoal strokes. Her hands

try to hide under her like hunted grouse.
As she draws even more into herself

hunched over her small pink breasts,
I see in her some resemblance

to myself. For hours she stares fixedly
at a spot in front of the pointed toes

of her incongruous shoes.

***

A slate-colored landscape is pressed
against the North Sea. From the beach café,

empty and lashed by rain, strings
of summer carnival flags hang limply.

A few black-backed gulls, roosting on
the sea wall, face into the wind

shedding the weather from their sleek
feathers. Suddenly I notice, on the terrace,

a large bronze woman sitting proudly
on a green metal bench. She is filling

herself with salt air. She is about to rise,
shake out the folds of her bronze draperies,

and stride down the beach to the sea.

Afterlife of the Ibis

I have been folded here
as if into a nest with my long bill,

slender and curved as an upholstery needle,
pressed against me. I have slept

many days under resinous wrappings
until woken by the piccolo notes

of green bee-eaters
flying, migrating overhead.

Trapped in this stone maze
it is cold and dark for a bird

that embodies all notions of light—
with a life-thread passing through pearls,

with bright mirrors embedded in its feathers,
and with a fierce desire to be plucked up

and out through the entrance shaft
by the humming wind

and quicksilver rivulets of the river
and return to my former haunts

where the water-birds are feeding.

If someone loves me, she will find me there.
She will search for my three-tined

toe tracks and intertwine
them with her own. Together

we will sew the horizon to the sky
with our thin curved bills.

Our calls will be low, resonant
far-carrying—*kraaa, kraaa.*

Angle of Light

We just needed different light effects.

We needed a change in the sun's angle
at the time it was striking the sliding glass door

and creating reflections that confused the two
Eurasian collared-doves that collided into it

and broke their necks. I went into the backyard,
to the other side of the glass, to see what

the doves saw, and saw that the outside
and inside appeared to exist on the same plane—

slivers of blue sky between the plum-tree
branches, and your astronomy calendar

on the kitchen wall, merged seamlessly together.

After you had slipped their bodies into Ziploc bags
and placed them side by side on the top shelf

of the freezer, above the frozen packets of
tortillas, you looked at them from time to time

to admire their dove-gray plumage,

their perfect markings.

Even weeks later, there remained on the glass
feathery smudges with a suggestion of wings.

But there was no need for you to worry.
Even in the welter of reflections

I still recognized you.

TWO

Uprooted

She runs through the broken china.
She runs through the shattered glassware of

her home. She runs carrying the tongues
of her five languages. She sees the long pink
tongues lolling out of the sides of the mouths

of dogs as they run behind her catching
the scent of her fear. She sees the small
unforgiving mouths of the guns. In the day

she turns into the shadow of an animal.
In the night she runs through the mud
of plowed fields, skirting all signs of habitation.

She crosses the borders—the ones that
are always changing. She crawls under

the barbed wire of several wars. She asks
the bushes why they can't make more shadow.

She asks the tongues of her five languages
why not one of them can help her. She asks

the crows—eddying over the fields
like the charred and blackened pages

of a great library—

whose side they are on.

Beach Races

We don't know if we've been entered
in the obstacle race or the hundred-yard sprint.

Either way we will start at the starting line, elbow
to elbow, a breeze whipping sand into our faces.

Either way the incoming tide will bring opalescent
jellyfish in to join the black wrack of seaweed

and the plovers will skitter along the shoreline
uttering their piping cries, as we run

on our short legs as fast as we can, our lungs
fluttering for breath. There will be a sky overhead,

and a sky underfoot reflected in the sheet
of wet sand—both marine-blue.

And the shallow lapping tide, green-blue.

As always my sister will cross the finish line first
and turn to flash a victory grin back at me

while a flag lifts and falls in the hands
of the umpire—a plump middle-aged woman,

whose name we will have forgotten.

On our periphery a string of beach donkeys
will stand by, ignoring us—heads down, quietly

flicking flies from their ears until one begins
to bray, startling us—a blaring cry

drawn up with great effort from the bottom
of its gut—wheezy snorts and urgent trumpets,

one after the other. We will not be sure

if it's a cry of relief or despair.

The Teacup

When she accidentally swept
the full teacup off the table
with one uncertain gesture, the wrens
in the garden broke into alarm calls.
They twitched in and out of the rose trellis
flicking their loosely-hinged tails.
The room became shadowy.
The ghost of her mind began crying.
As she looked down
the thick leafy hedge behind the roses
swallowed the wrens. She knew
there was no path back.

Berlin

Flanking the museum entrance
are two smoke-blackened, headless figures.

Their heads were lost in the war. Their
mouths are lying open somewhere

like small caves in the weeds.
Today, a heavy fog rolls between

the office blocks. If the statues could speak
their voices would be like the first hairs

of frost of a hard winter.

***

I am waiting on the edge of a bleak
construction site on which four zebra-striped

cement mixers are rotating smoothly
churning out their tonnage of cement.

Behind me on a billboard a giant hamburger
bun is dripping a waterfall of cheese
that coagulates in a sticky pool

at the level of my neck. A current
of windblown leaves splits around

glass-and-steel buildings. Hooded crows hop
sideways among flying fast-food wrappers.

From somewhere amidst the rubble
the authorities have transported the capital

of a neoclassical column and deposited
it among the flowerbeds and ornamental trees

of a city park. Lonely and bullet-pocked,
it is ignored by the troupe of red-capped children

running past it, kicking through the dry leaves.
Surrounded by stripped branches, facing winter,

perhaps I should dye my hair orange.
Perhaps sorrow will rise up

and disappear in my orange hair.

Voices of Nagasaki

The square seemed bigger than it used to be.
I tried to telephone the past from a lime-green

public telephone, but there was only
a busy signal embedded in static.

***

At that time, more than fifty years ago, there was
a shortage of everything. Mostly we lived on rice.

But I remember standing at night in the lantern-lit
grounds of the temple of Kannon—the deity

of mercy and compassion—eating octopus buns
with my wife. It was one of

the happiest times of my life.

***

After the world turned yellow I crouched under a
table. There was a noise like thunder,

and several miles away the cupboards fell over.
People were stumbling and dying

in the acrid yellow dust.

***

The city officials report it is painstaking work
to construct a map of the obliterated area

from the memories of survivors. It has taken all these
years, and still it is incomplete. After a while

the memories faded.

There are many empty spaces on the map.

***

There was glass everywhere. Black raindrops.

***

Since then the world has changed utterly.

There are only a few tatami makers left these days.

Enoshima Aquarium

How would it be to sleep all night
on a straw tatami mat, in a room of aquariums
containing bioluminescent jellyfish? To feel
the flexible bells opening and closing, opening
and closing, the tentacles waving
the touch of eerie blue-green rays?
Would my dreams be strange? Would
I have trouble falling asleep, stay awake
listening to the drumbeat of my heart
while the jellyfish continued bearing
their lights through the dark—
like so many marine Florence Nightingales
gliding through the wards, taking note of the dead,
comforting the desperately sick
and wounded lying on their cots?
Would I achieve tranquility? Make peace
with the cold white bodies floating
in the underwater cave of myself?
Reach some understanding
of Florence's brisk and brittle pragmatism—
the ability to choose, from among the thousands
of seriously wounded, which lives to try to save?
In the night she comes to offer solace.

In the day—urgently by telegraph to London—
she requisitions three hundred scrubbing brushes.

Nadya, Stalin's Wife

An agenda was necessary for the fifteenth
anniversary of the Revolution—an evening of
dancing, vodka and salted fish, maybe some lamb,

and, unusually flamboyant for her, she wore
a black dress embroidered with roses.

At the Black Sea dacha in May, sunlight poured
into the room. She opened a window

to jasmine and mimosa, immersed herself
in the songs of small birds. By October,

a whiff of starvation from the Ukraine. A betrayal,
she thought, but that was *his* business. Meanwhile
she had severe abdominal pains. Meanwhile

there were the comings and goings
of the operatives formulating their secret codes—

a coded crow perched on the Kremlin wall.

A coded rat fled across the apartment floor.

A coded woman, in that same embroidered dress, in
the early hours, put a bullet through her heart.

From the start the agenda was troubled—
some of the dinner guests arranged the liquidation

of others. Those who survived averted their eyes.
Those without cunning were doomed.

In the Kremlin gloom she had lost touch
with the rosefinches.

Red Crossbills

After the passengers
have abandoned their deckchairs
to the ice of the Atlantic wind,
a flock of red crossbills flutters
down onto the upper deck and runs
twittering among coils of rope
and iron winches. Over the horizon,
out of sight, an island juts up—
an island of moss
and volcanoes, dotted
with whalebones. Banners
flap on its stone pier.
And in the local bar
the members of the brass band
assembled to welcome us
are warming their hands, offering
toasts, tuning their instruments.
From the interior of the ship
the clatter of cutlery and
muffled conversations rise up,
as the deckchairs, sprawled
on the bitterly cold sundeck,
continue gliding through
the clarity of the north—legs askew
boldly striped canvas
ballooning out.

The Empress Elisabeth

Since her marriage at sixteen she has been
surrounded, stifled by the velvet curtains

of State. He is always punctilious, polite
and kind, but after the maid coiling and coiling

her hair, hour after hour, up into an elaborate
dark shell, she asks what is hers, if anything?

Not the Rose Brocade Room, nor
the Blue Porcelain Room. Certainly not the glassy
eyes of the deer heads staring from his walls.

Not even the lovely Greek temple, the Gloriette,
perched on its leafy hill above the oak woods.

Perhaps she has only memories of those woods—
the passageways of leaves stirred by wind
along which she will travel,

always without jewelry, always incognito—

crisscrossing the oceans of the world
accompanied by the drumming of woodpeckers,

still trying to make sense of her life.

A New Self

—Paula Modersohn-Becker (1876-1907)

Over fifty altogether, spread now
through various museums and private collections.

What was she looking for in all those selves?
She wakes early thinking of yellow plums,

wakes to a strong note of passion
from the ticking clock beside her—

another self tapping under the breastbone
a self with the bloom of plums.

Aloneness is necessary.
A wobbling orbit is necessary.

She must begin. She must mix her paints.
Intent, she leans forward paintbrush in hand

to create another self out of white space
and her fruitful essence.

A new face. A new Paula. She is pleased.

A clear light falls through the studio window.
The plums are quietly ripening in their bowl.

She is uncovering herself. She
has emerged at last—

pale, half-nude, and surprisingly pregnant
against a background of waxy laurel leaves.

Did she suspect, perhaps, that
that birth might erase her?

Joy Adamson with the Cheetah Cub, Pippa

Sleeping under the stars, she is
here beside me. As I breathe her exhaled breath
my hand falls against the spotted silk of her fur.

Tomorrow, if you happen to see me
as I sit in my lounge chair sipping
an evening cocktail, you may think I'm

on holiday on the Costa Del Sol—
mini-shorts, suntop, sandals, bleached blond
hair, stylishly arranged—but look again

you will see that I'm waiting for her to return.
You will see the shadows of red-rumped swallows
flickering overhead, and that I've picked up

my feet so as not to impede the migration
of snakes. The fact is: unbalanced, quarrelsome,

and anthropomorphic as I am, she is returning me
to the wild. Soon I will stop checking the thin,

Swiss-precision, gold watch that hangs loosely
on my wrist and I will fall out of her hands.

She, who I have loved always,
will fall out of my hands.

Visiting the Volcano

At the scenic viewpoint the volcano presented
itself in its most striking aspect—a perfect cone

standing by itself on level ground, the clouds
behind it tinted red by the sinking sun.

Warning notices demanded my full attention—
the dangers of unexpected fissures,
deep ash deposits, falling lava blocks.

And, though mostly asleep, the thin thread of fire
that may sometimes escape its lips—

You must proceed at your own risk.

I took a taxi to the parking lot, then climbed
its bare flank, purple-brown pebbles
skittering underfoot.

At the rim, I caught my breath, peered over
and recoiled—stunned by the deep black pit gaping
below me, its vertical walls hissing steam,
vapors swirling in its depths.

Not that I was afraid, but suddenly
I knew a biting solitude.

Where was she now the woman I loved?

At the hotel I chose a small corner table near
the window, ordered a light dinner, and ate alone.

As I swirled the clear red wine in my wine glass
I addressed my questions to it—

Could I possibly outrun a pyroclastic flow?
Definitely not.

What is the volcano trying to tell me?
*That the earth has many weak seams and they
can tear apart without warning.*

Can love be boundless?
*There are always boundaries but often
they are invisible.*

Woodpecker

In the garden of the woodpecker there
is a darkness that's hard to discuss.

In the bull terrier, Missy, it was
called a phantom pregnancy. She woke up

and it seemed to wriggle inside her. After
a few weeks it found a way out.

It was this that triggered the attack—

with her forty-two teeth she clamped
down on the boy's head and would not

release her grip, even when the mother
beat her fiercely on the back with a chair—
it was the nearest thing to hand.

The photo of Missy in the newspaper,
taken a week before she was put down,

is sandwiched between the scowling face
of a prisoner in the dock and an ad

for "Ultrasonex, the ultimate tooth whitener,"

illustrated by an open mouth
with two rows of perfectly white teeth.

In the garden of the woodpecker
a water dish for birds is balanced on a stack

of cement blocks. The house sparrows
and house finches come to drink and bathe

flying toward it through
the flickering shadows of the apple trees.

Like the woodpecker, I search the ground
under the trees, digging through the leaf-litter

to find my own grubs of darkness.
Then quickly rebury them because

they are too disquieting to swallow.

THREE

White Scarf

—A Photo. Jewish History Museum, Amsterdam

The wind comes from the north
and gathers strength across
the flatness of the polders. In the gray
light of dawn, trains slide over canals
carrying long ribbons of faces.
There are glimpses of life in the windows
of seventeenth-century houses.
In one, a vase of red tulips, in another
a woman lost in reflection combing her hair.
She pauses, her thoughts
caught in the black and white
net of the past.
There are no color photos.
A small knot of people stand
in a courtyard, pressed into a corner
between massive brick walls.
One arm is outstretched
like a white scarf in a plea
for ordinary life. A bleak
wind rattles the shutters. Faces
in the windows of the trains
float like small colorless tulips
held against the dawn.

Gibraltar

At night the little owls fly over the Pillars of Hercules
across the pitch-black strait, on migration to their
wintering grounds in Africa.

By day the sea becomes a blue mirror, streaked silver
where schools of flying fish leap to escape pursuing
dolphins. An undercurrent flows in its depths,

runs counter to the one at the surface—exits
through the mouth, stronger and saltier.

Tier upon tier, the town mounts the lower slopes
up into the *maquis*. Its rooftops have been

commandeered by yellow-legged gulls—they
stare over the neighborhood, preen studiously,

then tip back their heads to emit raucous
chuckling and gargling calls.

From Safeway I labor up three flights of ancient
stone steps, weighted with groceries.

The governor's residence is blindingly white—a
whiteness that serves to heighten the red and purple
of bougainvillea spilling over its walls.

In his tidy garden, caterpillars sheathed in green
satin change leaves into lace.

Some years the dwarf citrus tree bears fruit.

Some years it doesn't. The light is bone-deep.

In a barrel-vaulted dining room, among antique
furnishings, I drink coffee laced with vanilla.
My feelings are derived from the birds.

Far off to the west, a dark cloud of griffon vultures
drifts in haze. A blue rock thrush skitters
across the Mediterranean Steps.

Blows the Levanter—clouds drop onto the Rock
and migration is halted. At dawn you can see

the owls arrayed along the stone wall
of Princess Caroline's Battery, alert and immobile,

furred by mist.

The Caucasus 1999

Mechanic #3, the Oil Rocks, Baku.

Surrounded by rusty machinery, supported
by the scaffolding of the oil platform—

hair pulled back, graying at the edges, she
smiles while connecting the black rubber hose

to the industrial-sized showerhead, gold teeth
gleaming like fireflies in the rear of her mouth—

*Summer or winter, you see, we shower
with seawater. You see, in a nutshell
this is hard and dangerous terrain—this open deck*

*blistered by sun, a collapsing infrastructure,
my son murdered and thrown under a train.*

*But slowly you tune yourself to the lament
of the oil pumps, and once in a while, behind*

*their creaking pulse, you can hear the tiny
compassionate voices of fish swimming
along the edge of the platform—a choir of a kind.*

Sometimes, large flocks of migrant
white pelicans mark the direction of the wind.

***

Stalin's head is excavated. It is trussed up in ropes
and hoisted above ground by hydraulic winch.

The officials stand ramrod straight. The onlookers
cheer—*Perhaps now we will have electricity.*

***

Living over water, drinking from
the rust-stained river, they have forgotten some
of the arithmetic of erased names.

One discordant note has been broken into many,
filtering down through the chestnut trees.

In spite of everything the electricity fails.

Chernobyl

April 1986. I am standing in a stone circle in the Lake District while my father is taking photos and my mother is leaning against one of the gray Neolithic stones, arms folded, with a brooding look on her face. The stones, thirty-eight or forty, according to which ones are counted, are of a dense metamorphic rock and encrusted with rosettes of green and orange lichen.

Twelve miles to the south stands Dove Cottage—newly whitewashed by the Wordsworth Trust—and also St. Oswald's Churchyard where William's grave, together with Mary's, is marked by a plain headstone inscribed with their names and dates of death, and screened by the dark green foliage of a yew that William himself had planted earlier in his life. Dorothy is nearby.

Behind our guesthouse a mountain rears up steeply—a patchwork of heather, orange bracken and frost-shattered scree. White shapes of sheep are moving almost imperceptibly across it. On the guesthouse black-and-white TV, Chernobyl is a set piece—the fuzzy gray block of the damaged reactor, and an enormous stem of black smoke, almost solid, rising from it.

April is lambing season. Already the pregnant ewes
have been brought down from the upper pastures
to a nearby field to give birth. In the night I can hear
their quiet bleating.

Around the ruins of Reactor Number Four, soldiers
stroll with buckets picking up lumps of radioactive
graphite and nuclear fuel by hand, and tipping them
into metal containers.

In the Lake District—clashing air masses, torrential
rain.

In my dream, my mother is sitting in the rain on
a stone among the ruins of an ancient abbey, with
only a cheap plastic raincoat for a covering. A few
sheep are wandering around her, methodically
cropping the grass. Suddenly she tilts her head and
cups her ear. She says she thinks she can hear
thunder rolling out of nowhere.

I wake to discover that mist has dropped in the night
and covered the mountain. In white drifting bands
it circles the stone houses of the village, dampening
sound. In my mouth there is a metallic taste.

In a cemetery on the outskirts of Moscow
the radioactive dead of Chernobyl are buried in lead
coffins, soldered shut.

Catherine the Great Flying a Merlin

In this low-lying countryside
near St. Petersburg, I watch the clouds

shift and scatter over the birch woods,
the rough elbows of pine between the lakes.

A stocky dark falcon, she grasps
my gloved hand with bright yellow talons—

and I am bound to her—a tie
that's hard to explain given her

pugnacious disposition, the eyes that stare

straight through me into the distances

where she will fly with forceful piston-like
wing strokes—knifing the starling flock

into two separate throngs.

But out here, with her, each moment is clear.
Nothing needs to be justified or accounted for—

the stacks of documents on my desk,

the tiresome plotting of the boyars,

my task of annexing Poland
and consolidating my power.

How sharply defined, how perfect,
are the overlapping waves
of her streaked feathers.

Archway of Tears

—An elderly maidservant is consigned to the Birmingham
Union Workhouse, 1905.

If you should think of me, I am
entering here under the *Auspices of Charity*
through the Archway of Tears to join the fate

of the broken teapot, the dented bowl,
the rusty sieve. In front of me—
a discolored wall with a black

drainpipe slithering down its side,
a hundred starlings whistling

from its ledges. Overhead
the cast-iron bells are clanging—
"God is just, God is truth, God is love."

Are you my benefactor, O Lord?
Are the angels flying in airy circles above me,

above the grime, the sooty smokestacks,
the crumbling brick? Are they asking, "Emily,

for goodness sake, where have you
put the serviette holders, the cut-glass butter
dish, the ivy-patterned tureen?"

Ryazan

In postwar Britain it seemed that all public
buildings: hospitals, schools, swimming baths,

had the same interior color scheme—pea-green
on the lower third of the walls and a wan yellow
extending to the ceiling.

In the Age of Austerity there were long queues
everywhere, and a shortage of colors.

***

In this 1991 black-and-white photograph taken
at a hospital in Ryazan I imagine the scabby walls
in those same shades of yellow and green—

Four Russian women, broad and square,
stand, feet planted, in a room furnished with
two industrial-size sinks fed by antiquated taps.

The two visiting nurses are square also,
with capable square hands that hold clipboards

and comb through the hair of the four naked
women searching for the eggs or young of lice.

***

Sometimes, when you are crossing the rivers of
a bare and unforgiving landscape, you see

in the dusk those practical drab colors
waiting to rob you of your clothes.

You open your mouth and it fills

with the bitter cold of the steppes.

Notes of a Lesbian Physics Teacher

—England, 1956

While the girls are learning deportment
by circling the gym balancing books on their
heads, I draw a series of zeroes

on the blackboard—a series so long it slides
over the edge and extends along the wall.

I stand back. I ask myself—
Is this a representation of infinity?

Or the way I feel?

***

I ask you—if a mouse were rocketed into space
would it continue to run all night on its wheel
though night and gravity existed only in its head?

Or would it float about ghost-like, swiveling slowly,
its tail drifting like a thin pennant behind it?

***

I pluck white dead-nettles from the verge—
two-lipped, horn-shaped flowers
(dead meaning only that they are non-stinging)

I continue in dead silence
(dead meaning only that I admit nothing.)

***

This love could have been a copse hammering
with woodpeckers. It could have been
a water-meadow flecked with cinquefoil.

As we turned the pages to the color plates
our hands brushed, hovering
above the yellow flame of the wild iris—

as if I didn't have a position to keep

as if I didn't have a position to keep.

***

Before me, bent heads of the girls staring
into their notebooks, hard-pressed to answer

the questions I have set. They are trying
to visualize a clock of circling figurines

flying at the speed of light
or Einstein's elevator falling through emptiness.

***

I myself have become a dead weight
meaning—I am falling farther than the girls
in their red and navy uniforms

meaning, as the stars plummet through the air
they turn to scrap-metal.

After the Accident

While my mother lies stiffly
on her back in the hospital,
low-spirited, with a compound fracture

of the ankle, I wander through the city's
shopping malls, from one security camera

to another—on each screen appearing
grainier and more distracted.

A dog in a backyard barks disconsolately.
At my mother's bedside the nurses apologize—
they don't have time. And they are underpaid.

Three blocks from the cathedral
in a third-floor hotel room, drab and cramped—
(bed, washbasin, towel rack)

I ponder a window's rectangle
of clouded sky, the trajectories

of pigeons flying across it.

Saturn's Rings

She who was born between the wars
and had escaped south out of
the Great Depression with a fiery streak
in her hair, now finds herself

standing in the entryway of her house
excavating the contents of her handbag—
not once, but three times—searching
for whatever it was she thought
she needed to retrieve.

She looks up with a rueful smile. Last night,
by spacecraft, from 900 million miles away, images
of Saturn's rings had arrived on her TV—and
they looked familiar. Something akin

to interference, or perhaps the ribbons of shadow
thrown across her kitchen counter by the loose
branches of the weeping willow.

But still—so much of the world seems
to be speaking to her in code—in ring tones
and electronic beeps and little
flashing red and green lights, while she,

a woman from the time of horses,
must pause, listen again
for the steady clip-clop of hooves.

John Edward

At last he climbs out of the trenches with a few
body lice and a hoarse whisper in his throat.

Look, she says, *I have gathered together*
two armchairs, a black iron fireplace
and a budgerigar

in a bell-shaped cage—
You must make yourself at home.

And pulling a large handkerchief
from her apron pocket, she sneezes

into it, releasing into the room the scent
of her spiced snuff—a fragrant cloud of nutmeg

and cloves that mingles with the acrid
blue smoke of smoldering coals in the grate.

The budgerigar emits a cheerful chirp,
wipes its beak on a shard of cuttlefish bone

and John Edward falls asleep
in his armchair, climbs down once again

into the darkness where war hovers.

Anna

—More than a hundred people, mostly elderly women,
inhabit Chernobyl's 30-km. Zone of Alienation.

Anna laughs through the gaps
of her lost teeth as she stirs a pot of chicken broth,
her hands appearing and disappearing

in a cloud of steam. On the wooden table—
a brown loaf, slices of white pig fat, horseradish
roots in a chipped blue bowl.

Why did you return?

A dove never strays far from her nest.

Subzero winters. But spring comes
with white anemones and storks build their
massive nests on our telephone poles.

Our night music is the long howling of wolves.

Look—the animals thrive here. They are our
witnesses.

And, as if ready to testify, outside the window,
a small group of roe deer on the far side

of the marsh, step out into the open
from the shadow of the birches.

Reactor Number Four sulks
in its cracked steel-and-concrete sarcophagus
slowly leaking alpha and beta particles into the air.

Some people think this land is cursed.

But even a half-wild pig
will return to root in its own yard.

The Cherry Tree

A young woman, a dog and a cherry tree
stand at the edge of the lawn, just this side
of the property line marked by a six-foot tall hedge.

The cherry tree holds still, caught between
its blossoming and fruiting. The young woman,

in her moss-green dress, is pale and unsmiling.
Perhaps she is thinking—I want to leave

home and begin a new life. But she is fixed
in this garden, bound to the cherry tree,

and the dog, to the camera's glassy eye,
and a sky tufted with white cloud. Under her touch

the dog is still—gray-muzzled, cloudy-eyed,
with front legs bowed out like those

of a Queen Anne dresser. A flock of pigeons sweeps
overhead. Beneath the lawn the tree's roots fan out

like a peacock's tail. Next door, behind the hedge,
the sound of Mrs. Wilcox watering her laburnums.

If I could put my ear to the cherry tree's
gray trunk I could hear water gurgling upward

in a million tiny tubes, pulled by thirsty leaves.

If I could put my ear to the ground I could hear
the burrowing earthworms passing the dark heart
of the earth through their bodies.

The camera blinks. An image is recorded.
The dog hobbles away. The cherry tree

perseveres and inherits the garden. Year after year
it reaches for the sky—solitary and bereft—

one half of its trunk coated with green algae.

FOUR

Return

When I returned I didn't know whether
to follow the soft cooing of the white-winged dove

or the bleating call of the collared dove—they
were both there among the leaves.

But a blue-overalled woman stocking
the lower shelves of the local supermarket

advised me which way to go—and soon
her directions sorted themselves into left and right.

It was a large austere building, the hospital
that was also an asylum, located on a hill
overlooking the long body of a lake.

Hard wooden benches lined the outer wall
on which the patients, on warm days,
sometimes sat or slumped—

silent and withdrawn, for how
could they think when their thoughts
were tangled like clumps of waterweed?

And how could they speak if no one was listening?

Below them, the lake was an inverted sky
plied by small white clouds like boats—

the lake, that some said,
produced thoughts of suicide.

When I returned I found I was the only visitor.
All the patients had vanished,
together with their illnesses

and their medical records.

Below me the lake was like the body
of a dead kingfisher—the one I had discovered
in my garden earlier in the year, its feathers

a mat of blue silk. That it was a sign
I had no doubt. Just as the doves were a sign
each speaking to me of loss.

Goldfish

Where two children find solace in a dog,
where an exhausted racing pigeon
drowns in the rainwater vat—
a gray rag with a leg ring—

and two adults battle it out
with shrill voices and slammed doors
and the crabapple tree leans as if fatigued—

two goldfish circle for years in a glass tank
quietly finning through bubble-streams
and Canadian pondweed, above a pink shipwreck
sunk in bacteria-free gravel.

The room's décor is decorative. Where a carpet
of one pattern runs up against wallpaper
of a discordant pattern, conflict is inevitable.

Taut faces. Thickened air.
Someone needs to draw up a treaty.

Dear goldfish—two half-empty cups
and a cold teapot sit abandoned in the kitchen
while a red carpet of repetitive ribbons of roses
is sliding under our feet—

Already we are listing. Help!
Are the lifeboats ready?

The goldfish keep swimming.
They are gold threads in the mouth of
a seamstress working at her table.

The tablecloth comes and goes,
covering or uncovering, shielding or not shielding,
billowing or slumping.

At the Garden Center

The garden center damp with breath
of the nearby canal. Bare light bulbs. Quivering
tinsel. Even in her blue coat

and with her handbag over her arm,
she is feeling cold. So in a back corner,
somewhat protected, we sit at a round table

sipping tea out of paper cups surrounded
by owls, gnomes, hedgehogs, mushrooms,
and buddhas, set out on the concrete floor,

green price tags attached—
as if we are part of a bizarre fairy tale.

***

The mother says to the floor—
I'm not quite ready for the bone-pile yet.
And the tinsel flickers in agreement.

The daughter says to the table, while studying
the blue cables of veins crossing her mother's
hands—*You've pulled strongly my whole life.*

And the gnomes cross-legged on toadstools
nod their assent. And the weeds outside
in the fields stand up straight, stiff with frost.

***

So silence travels slowly
across the table between us. In it we can hear

the poinsettias murmuring as they take
small sips of water into their leaves.

And the voice of the canal growing hoarse
as it slides under the bridge.

The Beach at Trouville

—Claude Monet, 1870

The two women on the beach
probably Camille and Mme. Boudin

are sitting on wicker chairs, reading
under the blue shadows of their parasols.

They sit as if they are passengers in
this landscape, close but separate

in their hooped skirts, an empty chair
between them, their parasols like starfish

against a pearly, cloud-brushed sky.
Later, this particular afternoon

of quiet friendship will come back to them—
such deep breaths of briny air. And

the expanse of the sea—immense, behind
the bright defiant flowers of Camille's hat.

The Ladies of Llangollen

Of the forty-four varieties of roses, of
the winding, raked gravel paths, of the Gothic bird
cote, there appears to be no sign.

In front of their house, now open to visitors, I see
a formal topiary of dark green, clipped shapes
(Eleanor in particular would have disliked it
and objected vociferously)
They preferred a garden
of carefully planned wildness—
romantic tree-framed vistas, growths of moss
and ferns, stones decorated by the mottling
effects of age and the forces of nature.

Under the Gothic and Tudor trappings,
added by themselves and others, there stands
the plain square stone cottage
with a slate roof where they settled in 1780—
after their scandalous flight together from Ireland,

changing its name from *Pen-y-Maes*
to *Plas Newydd* (the New Place),
busying themselves, as income allowed,
with draperies, bookcases, arches, rustic bridges,
and improving their minds, and—
in their happiness—

wandering out in the moonlight
to visit their cow, Margaret.

I think of those long cold Welsh winters—their
burlap sacks of coal stacked high
in the cellar, snow trapping the coaches
on the Horseshoe Pass, nights illuminated

by best-quality Windsor Soap candles
ordered from Oswestry,

Eleanor with her satiric tongue, by turns haughty
and generous, constantly dismissing
then re-employing the same servants.

Fifty years together. Sarah leads Eleanor, tottering
and blind with cataracts,
through the oak-paneled library
upstairs to their beloved four-poster,
where Mrs. Silk purrs on the coverlet.

In polite society the exact nature
of their relationship became the subject of talk.

In the Vale they were known simply
as *The Ladies*.

Last Days

A day of solid rain.
All her nightdresses have been washed and dried
but hoarse breathing troubles the room.

In the garden, three blackbirds square
off in the apple tree—lifting their yellow beaks
into the air, glaring with gold-rimmed eyes,
clucking, chuckling,

contending for the glut of mealy red apples
still clipped to winter-black branches.

Rain rattles against the windows.
And, played to an unfamiliar tune by
a relief organist, *Breathe on me, breath of God*,
turns out to be onerous—

the mourners' voices thin
and falter as they attempt to forestall
the unexpected rise and fall of notes.

Then, in brittle silence, at the flip of a switch,
the floor-to-ceiling, electrically-controlled curtains
sweep shut
and the coffin disappears from view.

In the night I think I can hear her
digging her own hole in the tough heavy
boulder-clay—flicking aside pebbles,
scrabbling with brown-spotted hands, while

the blackbirds sleep, their feet automatically
locked to their perches—a trick
that prevents them toppling off.

But one has dropped softly,
like a rain-soaked apple
to the spongy leaf-layer below.

A Short History

At first there were small upright
slabs of local red sandstone,

hand-hewn, warm to the touch
carved with the common emblems of mortality—

the hourglass, the scythe, the winged death's
head, or the snake—depicted with

a stinger in its tail or mouth
or sometimes grasping an apple.

Then the Victorians arrived
with their penchant for urns and doves

and elaborate monuments
chiseled from white Italian marble—

and the graveyards began bristling
with giant three-dimensional crosses, obelisks,

gesturing angels, mausoleums,
all heaving themselves heavenward—

a breathtaking display, particularly
when viewed against the sunset.

But still, I find myself turning
to contemplate the narrow waist of the estuary
funneling the sand grains slowly, steadily,

between shifting banks of
dune grass and sea lavender.

And the snake too—I remember it quietly
sunning its lithe, zigzag-patterned body

on a smooth slab of stone
among the blackberry bushes.

Viewing the Photographs

A tidy pile of fish bones, green olive pits
in a bowl, the curled peel of an orange,

a wrinkled white napkin balanced
delicately on the table like a floating swan.

It is as if they had just left. As if
they had just finished their meal and left
and were taking to the road again.

Perhaps, *this* road—this dusty road
bordered by walls of giant prickly pear,

a blaze of noon light sliding off their flat pads,
a horizon blurred through windshield glare,

and the triangle of her elbow resting
on the open window.

Up ahead the the road disappears into gray sky,
the desert is sown with stones.

But, it seems after someone dies
you see the photographs differently—

even the landscape appears
to be brushed by grief.

Gertrude and Alice

—Piazza San Marco, Venice

They had met and that was enough.
Through the cyclone of pigeons they emerge

as loving companions: Gertrude scattering
largesse in the form of millet seed—

voluminous and fully herself, a pigeon
balanced on each outstretched hand—
as in an astonishing circus act. Alice behind her,

delicate and heedful, the limp reticule
that dangles from her arm, retiring
into the folds of her dark batik dress.

Passion had announced itself and that
was enough. The waters of the Baroque fountain
had leapt in welcome, exuberant fake flowers

had come to encircle Gertrude's hat. It is 1908.
The pigeons elbowing around their feet are extras.

In the background—a small boy in a wrinkled
linen suit, stands staring, transfixed.

Lamy, New Mexico

An icy wind blows across the snakeweed flats
between juniper-dotted escarpments.

The restaurant is closed, the train station
deserted. As the eastbound Amtrack pulls in

a large flock of red-winged blackbirds flies up
from a clump of trees and circles—a handful

of black pebbles against the bleached sky.
No one gets on or off the train.

When the blackbirds settle again
in the upper branches of the box elders,

they begin a startling chorus—a rolling
squeaky melody that's the only sound besides

the subdued sighing of the waiting train.

When the train slides off again eastward
the station is as desolate as before.

Only the blackbirds, now silent, remain.

Saline Valley, December 29, 1936

*—Annie Alexander, field biologist, spent her 69th birthday
with her partner, Louise Kellogg, snowbound northwest of
Death Valley.*

In this deep sink between desert ranges
in this arid basin called Saline Valley

Louise and I wait out the storm. Mornings we split
wood in the wash, afternoons I add

to my field notes. Small mammals are always
uppermost in our minds. We stopped to look

for gopher sign in Waucoba Wash and again
in Marble Canyon. At that time there was snow
only on the highest peaks.

Now both access roads are blocked
and we are down to beans and cornmeal.

Fifteen-foot snowdrifts fill the upper canyons.
We have stopped washing dishes.

Before breakfast, as the temperature
hovered around zero, Louise struggled to light
the campstove, to blow life into wisps of flame.

This December seems particularly severe.
The ridges and basins are iron-hard

and the warrens of the gophers are like tunnels
of warm-blooded life under a frozen lid of soil.

Today is my birthday. I watch out for new species
of grass. I consider the 60s a very appropriate period
in one's life to do fieldwork.
I have learned to observe—

to distinguish the slightest variations
of color and form.

And we are not unhappy. In these remote places
that have become our territory,
we thrive, loving what little there is.

Keynotes

Caught in a live barrel trap the bear
makes a moaning sound that comes from
deep within her body, from the raw edge

of her fear, from the mossy roots
of the primeval forest before it was cut.

Lately I am beginning to hear voices.
I am beginning to hear the black holes

in outer space singing in B-flat—though
their song is fifty-seven octaves

below the level of human hearing. It is fall—

the river is slowing into ice, the rain
is thickening into snow. Everyone knows

it's been a poor berry crop this year,
the pink and silver salmon runs lower
than normal, not reaching as far inland.

She had broken canines. She needed
to put on more fat for the winter.

So it is time for the Fantasia. In the cold
hall the clarinetist stretches her mouth

and blows into her hands. It is time
for the trumpets, then the shaking of water

out of the instruments. High overhead,
surging south in the dark—currents

of small birds—warblers, thrushes, flycatchers,
keep in contact with a medley
of cheeps, chirps, and whistles.

I am sleeping with the window open,
ears open. I wonder, was it the bear visiting

the garbage cans or the hardening of the river
that set all the dogs barking again?

Travelers

You are there, floating in the weightless
flicker of the TV, focused on the rise and fall

of TV lives. You are following them, a small
boat pitching on the swells—those characters

that seem as real as anyone you know—

concentrated, leaning forward on the edge
of your worn velour chair, your face

netted with light.

***

I am here, far off, deciphering the faint
scars of animal tracks, marking my passage

with stone ducks in a tundra without
landmarks, in a disorienting vastness.

I am learning to recognize the individual

in the features that repeat themselves—
the rickrack of stones, the crusts of lichen,

the pensive songs of warblers circling
up from the willow scrub

and the coils of wind that tie
the packages of stones together. And at night

I find my bearings by the net of stars.

Notes

"After the July Bombings": On July 7, 2005, suicide bombers detonated bombs on four London Underground trains during the morning rush hour.

"Visiting the Earl of Dudley's Estate": The 18th-century mansion, and its parkland, formerly owned by the Earls of Dudley, was opened to the public in 1968.

"Self Portraits": This poem is based on two artworks—*Study for the Three Graces III,* a pastel and charcoal drawing on paper by Ana Maria Pacheco, and *Draped Seated Woman,* a bronze statue by Henry Moore.

"Afterlife of the Ibis": In ancient Egypt the ibis hieroglyph was the root hieroglyph for light. A mummified red-dyed ibis was sometimes placed in a tomb.

"Voices of Nagasaki": Some of the material in this poem was suggested by *Nagasaki Stories,* a film by Jos de Putter, Netherlands 1996.

"Enoshima Aquarium": This aquarium near Tokyo offers popular night retreats for those in search of inner peace.

"A New Self": The German expressionist painter, Paula Modersohn-Becker, died of an embolism at age 31 after giving birth to her first child.

"Joy Adamson with the Cheetah Cub, Pippa": Best known for her epic, *Born Free*, about the lioness she and her husband returned to the wild, Joy Adamson subsequently worked by herself on returning to the bush an eight-month old cheetah cub that had been raised as a pet.

"Woodpecker": This woodpecker is a Red-shafted Flicker. Unlike most woodpeckers it frequently forages on the ground.

"The Caucasus 1999": Some of the material in this poem was suggested by *On the Edge of Time—Male Domains in the Caucasus*, a film by Stefan Tolz, Germany 2001.

"Chernobyl": In April 1986, as the plume from Chernobyl traveled east over Britain it met with a storm front from the west. Heavy rain carried radioactivity into the soil. Mountain sheep continued to be monitored for radioactivity as late as 2012.

"John Edward": My grandfather, John Edward Mulholland. 1896-1956.

"Anna": This poem was written after viewing "Chernobyl, Still Life in the Zone," an exhibition by photographer Rena Effendi.

"The Ladies of Llangollen": Eleanor Butler and Sarah Ponsonby, two upper-class women from Ireland, lived together in a "romantic friendship," from 1778 to 1829, near the small town of Llangollen in Wales.

"Viewing the Photographs": This poem was written after viewing the exhibition—"Annie Leibovitz: A Photographer's Life 1990-2005." The exhibition was haunted by photographs of Susan Sontag who died in December 2004.

"Saline Valley, December 29, 1936": The material in this poem is based on Annie Alexander's correspondence, archived at the Bancroft Library, University of California, Berkeley.

"Keynotes": The Fantasia is Hadyn's *Fantasia in C Major.*

ACKNOWLEDGMENTS

My thanks to the editors of the following publications in which these poems first appeared, some in earlier versions:

Calyx: "Uprooted"
The Common Ground Review: "A Short History"
Conditions: "Saline Valley"
Earth's Daughters: "Afterlife," "Angle of Light"
The Literary Bohemian: "Berlin"
Pirene's Fountain: "After the July Bombings,"
    "Viewing the Photographs," "Ryazan"
Poetry Now: "The Teacup," "Saturn's Rings"
The Sow's Ear Poetry Review: "Enoshima Aquarium,"
    "At the Garden Center"
Stanislaus Connections: "Tyneside," "White Scarf"
Third Wednesday: "The Beach"
Tule Review: "Keynotes"

Many thanks to my teachers—Julie Bruck, James Arthur, and Ellen Bass, whose guidance and encouragement have nourished and shaped these poems.

And my deepest gratitude to the members of the Word Project Press team. Without their support and dedication this collection would not have been possible.

Sy Margaret Baldwin was born and raised in the West Midlands of England but has spent most of her adult life in California. Presently she lives in the Sierra Nevada. From 1992 to 2008 she worked as a Wildlife Technician for Stanislaus National Forest.

www.ingramcontent.com/pod-product-compliance
Lightning Source LLC
Chambersburg PA
CBHW060114050426
42448CB00010B/1867